EXTREME FASHION

Claire Llewellyn

Illustrated by **Fermín Solís and J**

OXFORD
UNIVERSITY PRESS

Contents

What is Fashion?

Clothes never stay the same for long. They are always changing. One year, everyone is wearing **drainpipe** trousers. Then a new fashion arrives. People stop wearing drainpipe trousers and start wearing **flared** trousers. Finally, fashion changes back again!

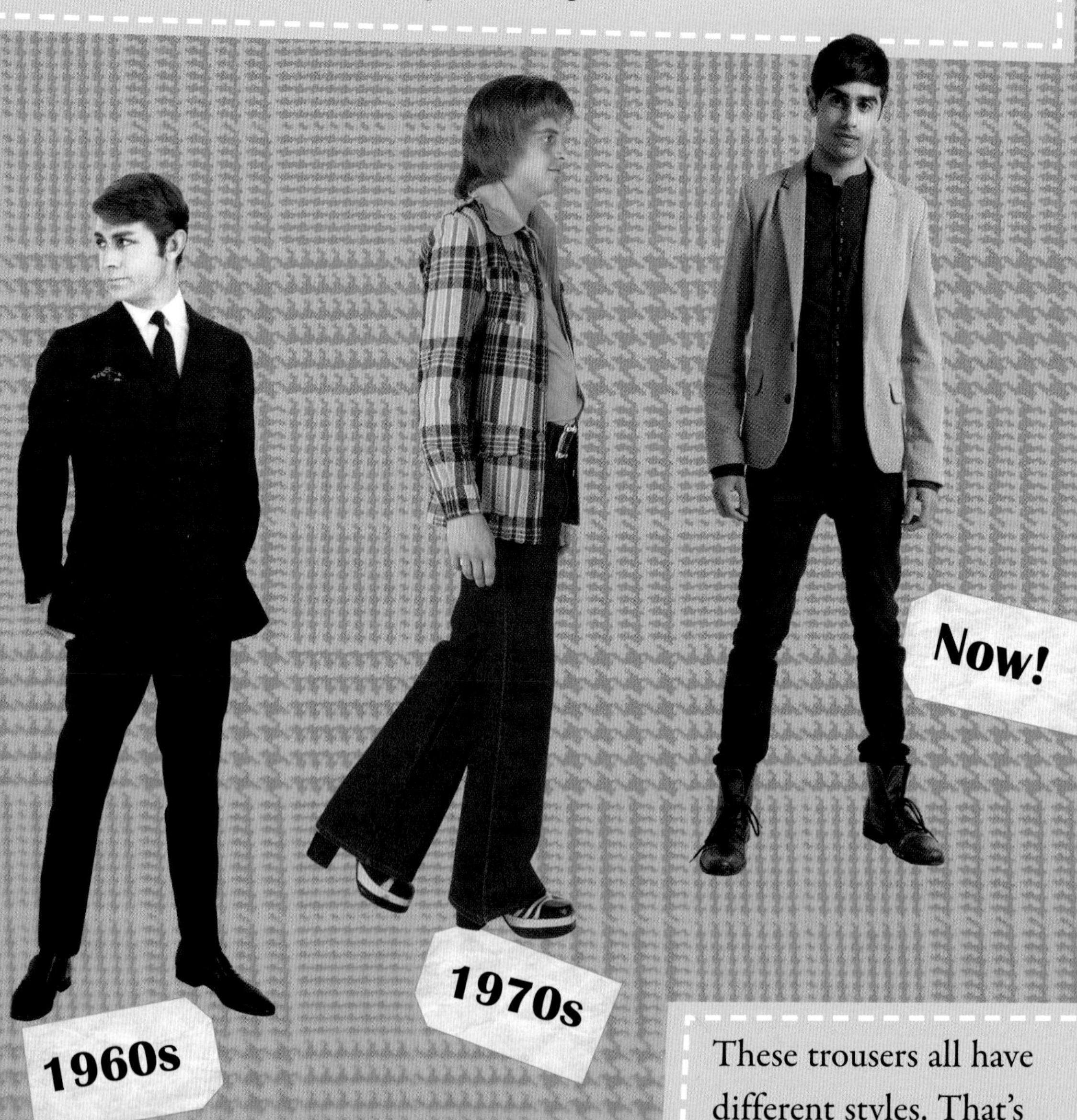

These trousers all have different styles. That's fashion!

Some fashions are shocking. Let's look at some of the strangest styles from the last 500 years. From the top of your head all the way down to your feet, this is extreme fashion!

A farthingale skirt

Thom Browne Autumn 2014 menswear collection

A Proud Head

About 500 years ago, rich people wore wide, frilly collars called ruffs. They were made of **linen fabric** folded into **pleats**.

The Servant's Handbook: Washing a Ruff

White ruffs get very dirty. Wash them every day.

1. Carefully wash the ruff with soap.
2. Use **starch** to make the fabric stiff.
3. While the ruff is damp, use hot sticks to put the pleats back into shape.

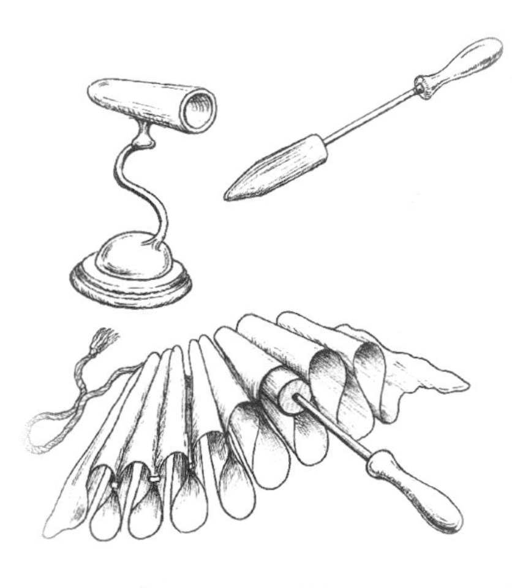

2000

A Perfect Face

In the 1500s, Queen Elizabeth I began to wear masks to protect her face. Other fine ladies followed her example. The masks were made of **silk** or **velvet**.

They had holes cut in them for the eyes. Ladies wore them to protect their faces from dust, wind and sun. The masks kept their skin soft.

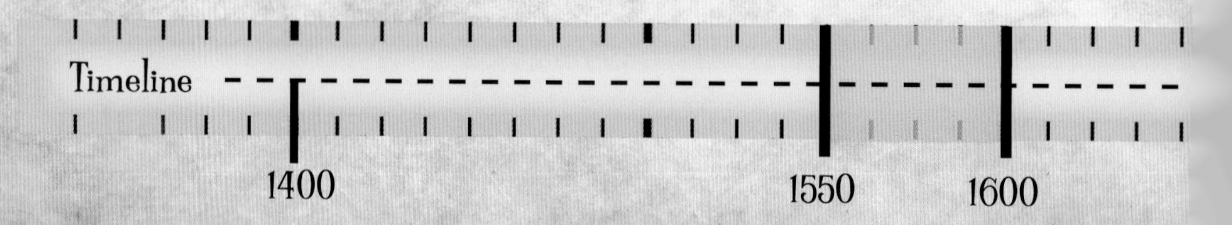

Many **Elizabethan** people had very bad skin. They often stuck patches onto their faces to hide spots and scars.

Hate your spots and scars?
Cover them with our
black silk patches.
Choose from four fashionable shapes:
sun, moon, heart or star.

Look fabulous in just one minute!

2000

A Strong Chest

In the 1500s, men wore tight jackets called **doublets**. Bones and **padding** were used to stiffen the jacket. Doublets gave the body a stiff, muscular shape.

There was only one problem: you couldn't bend over!

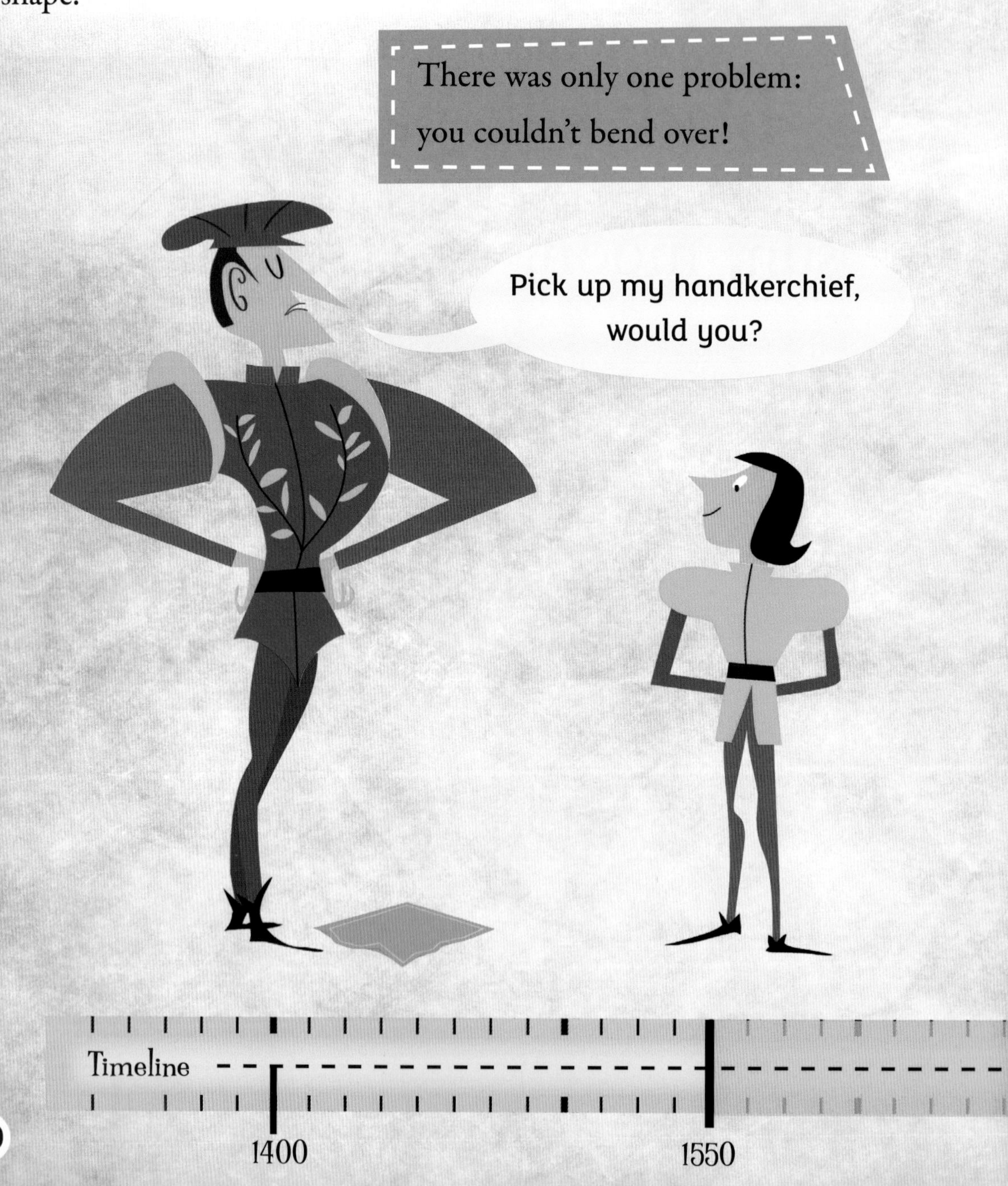

The sleeves of the doublet were padded. This made it difficult for men to move their arms.

Tailors had to add ready-made bends to the sleeves!

A Tiny Waist

About 250 years ago, women wore tight corsets under their clothes. A corset pulled in the tummy to make a tiny waist.

laces give the corset a tight fit

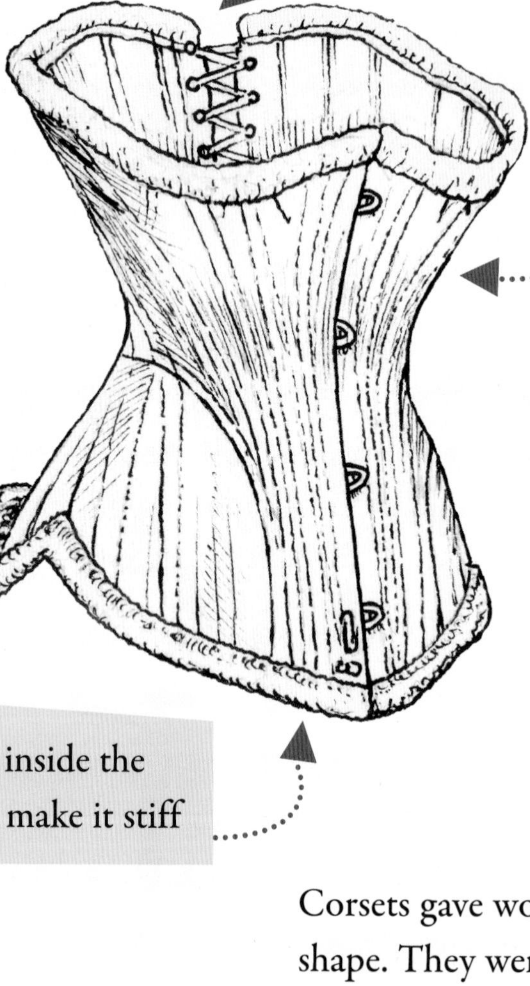

stiff fabric gives the corset a smooth curve

bones inside the corset make it stiff

Corsets gave women a curvy shape. They were popular for hundreds of years.

Timeline

1400

1600

Women wearing corsets could hardly breathe. They **fainted** easily and had stomach aches. Their muscles grew weak, which was bad for their backs.

Padded Hips

In the 1500s, fashionable men wore short, padded trousers. They were called hose. At that time, big hips were cool. The more padding you had in your hose, the better!

NEW-LOOK PADDED HOSE!
Padded hose stick out from waist to thigh.

They show off the legs while standing, dancing or bowing.

Padded hose also act as a cushion!

Timeline

1400

1550

The Sad Story of the Padded Hose

A fashionable gentleman wanted the biggest hose.

So he asked his tailor to stuff them with **bran**.

He was very proud of his padded hose.

Sadly, he didn't see a sharp nail on his chair ... or the bran spilling onto the floor!

1750

2000

Bottom Heavy

For about 300 years, it was fashionable for women to have wide skirts. From about 1850, they wore metal cages under their skirts. These cages were called crinolines. They made skirts stick out.

A crinoline was made of steel hoops. The hoops were held together with tape.

Timeline

1400 1600

CRINOLINES: A SILLY FASHION?

They take up space in carriages and trains.

They knock things over.

They catch fire easily.

They get caught in wheels.

1850 1870 2000

Shocking Legs

Until the 1900s, women's legs were always hidden by long skirts. So it was a **scandal** when women started wearing trousers. Everyone thought trousers were men's clothes. They were shocked to see a woman's legs, even though they were still covered up.

100 years of change

1900s

Women wear short **Turkish trousers** to ride their bikes.

1930s

A film star, Marlene Dietrich, has her photo taken wearing trousers.

Timeline

1400

1960s

Women still wear skirts to work. Many prefer trousers at home.

2000s

Most girls and women can now wear trousers to school or work.

1900 1930 1960 2000

Feet off the Ground

Platform shoes have very thick **soles**. They have been made and worn for hundreds of years.

Made in Spain from leather and cork in the 1400s

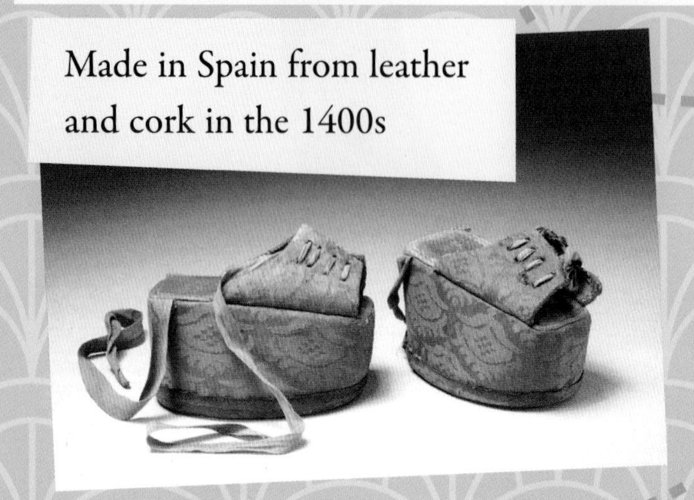

Wooden shoes made in Syria in the 1800s

Made in Italy from leather and cork in the 1930s

Made in Italy from snakeskin in 2010

Timeline

1400

We love platform shoes!

They lift me out of the mud and dirt.

The thick soles protect my feet from stones.

They make me look taller.

But not everyone does!

I'm afraid of heights!

Some fashions are just *too* extreme!

1800

1930

2010

Glossary

bran: outer covering of wheat which is left over when wheat is made into flour

doublets: tight jackets worn by men

drainpipe: very narrow

Elizabethan: relating to the time of Queen Elizabeth I

fainted: became unconscious for a short time

flared: very wide

linen fabric: fine material made from a plant called flax

padding: material stuffed into something to make it look bigger

pleats: folds in material

scandal: behaviour or event that people think is wrong

silk: fine, soft, shiny material

soles: parts of your shoes that you walk on

starch: special product that makes material stiffer

tailors: people who make clothes

Turkish trousers: wide trousers bunched below the knee, used by women for cycling and other sports

velvet: soft, thick material that is used to make fine clothes

Index

About the Author

I've been writing books for many years. Some of them are story books, but most of them are about real things like volcanoes or the Moon. I enjoy my job because I find out lots of stuff which I didn't know before.

I loved finding out about extreme fashion. What made perfectly sensible people wear padded hose? Couldn't they see how daft they looked? Hmm, that makes me wonder: what will people in the future think about the things we wear today?

Greg Foot, Series Editor

I've loved science ever since the day I took my papier mâché volcano into school. I filled it with far too much baking powder, vinegar and red food colouring, and WHOOSH! I covered the classroom ceiling in red goo. Now I've got the best job in the world: I present TV shows for the BBC, answer kids' science questions on YouTube, and make huge explosions on stage at festivals!

Working on TreeTops inFact has been great fun. There are so many brilliant books, and guess what ... they're all packed full of awesome facts! What's your favourite?